ECOCRAFTS

Jazzy
Jewellery

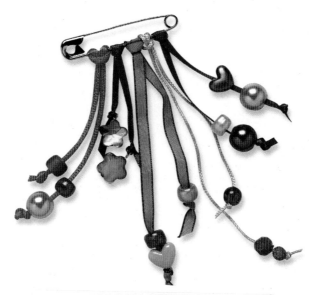

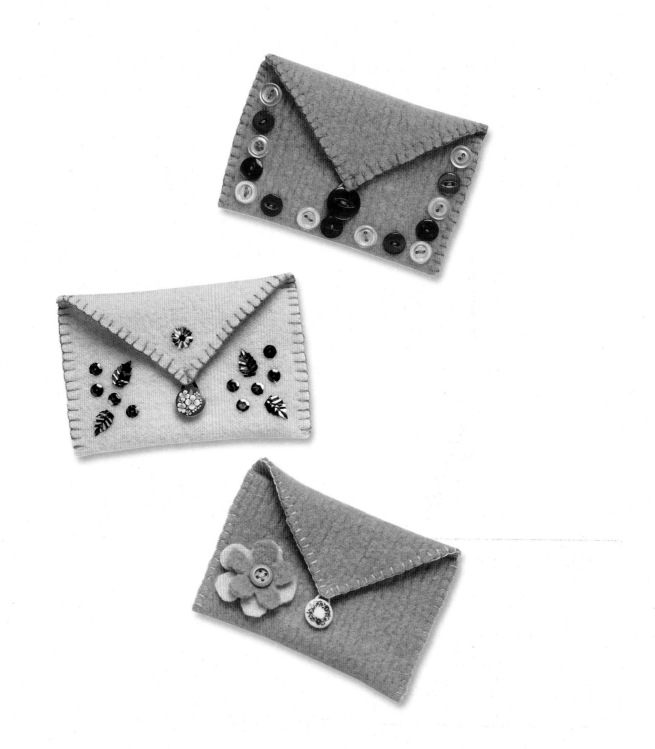

ECOCRAFTS
Jazzy
Jewellery

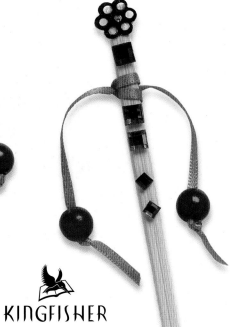

KINGFISHER

KINGFISHER

Kingfisher Publications Plc
New Penderel House
283–288 High Holborn
London WC1V 7HZ
www.kingfisherpub.com

First published by Kingfisher Publications Plc 2007
10 9 8 7 6 5 4 3 2 1
1TR/0507/C&C/MAR(MAR)/128OJIEX-GREEN/C

Authors: Dawn Brend, Kirsty Neale,
Cheryl Owen, Melanie Williams

For Toucan
Editor: Theresa Bebbington
Designer: Leah Germann
Photography Art Direction: Jane Thomas
Photographer: Andy Crawford
Editorial Director: Ellen Dupont

For Kingfisher
Senior Editor: Catherine Brereton
Art Director: Mike Davis
Senior Production Controller: Lindsey Scott
DTP Coordinator: Catherine Hibbert

A CIP catalogue record for this book
is available from the British Library.

ISBN 978 07534 1482 8

Printed in China

**The paper used for the cover and text pages is
made from 100% recycled post-consumer waste.**

Contents

Eco-wise

It's amazing what you can find around the house that you'll be able to turn into jewellery. By making your own jewellery, you make sure that it will be special to you – no one else will have jewellery that is exactly the same as the items you make.

As well as being really special, all the projects in this book help the environment by using everyday things found in your home. A lot of them are things you would have thrown away. You'll find ways to turn drinking straws into a bracelet, reuse bottle caps to make a necklace, create a handbag using gift wrapping paper and even use chopsticks to make your very own hair sticks. Recycling helps the planet because it reuses things that would have ended up in the dustbin.

Around the world tonnes of rubbish ends up in landfills each year. In the UK alone, we

3 'R's to recycling

About half of the rubbish in our dustbins can be recycled. Follow these steps to help prevent rubbish being sent to landfills or incinerators.

REDUCE – Encourage your parents to buy products that have little or no packaging.
REUSE – Find new ways to use jars, tins, plastic containers and other durable things.
RECYCLE – If you can't reuse something but it can be recycled, help your parents recycle it.

dump 28 million tonnes of household rubbish into landfills every year. This rubbish weighs the same amount as three-and-a-half million double-decker buses. If you lined up all these buses, they would wrap around Earth two-and-a-half times. Each year we create more rubbish than the year before, and if we continue to do so, it's thought that we'll double the amount of rubbish we produce by 2020.

When we throw away so much rubbish, we are also throwing away valuable resources. If we recycle our rubbish, fewer materials will need to be mined, quarried or grown, and less energy is used to transport these materials around the world. Another concern is that the landfills where rubbish is buried are filling up – and there's little space left to make new landfills.

What you can do

Save your buttons! Remove them from old clothes that are about to be used for rags. And look for extra buttons that come with new clothes. Buttons are great for making into jewellery.

Look for old jewellery in car boot sales and charity shops. This way you'll be helping to reuse things that would otherwise go to a landfill.

Take your old jewellery to a charity shop so it can be reused by someone else.

Save beads, gems and other trinkets from broken jewellery that can't be repaired. Use them to make your own new jewellery.

Pass on old jewellery that you no longer like to friends and family who might like them.

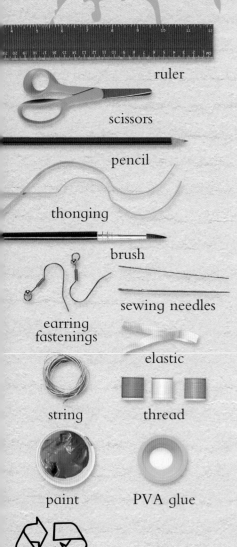

ruler

scissors

pencil

thonging

brush

sewing needles

earring fastenings

elastic

string

thread

paint

PVA glue

Getting started

Before starting a project, make sure you have everything you need. You will sometimes have to make a knot or do some sewing. If you're not sure how to do these, follow the steps here. Some craft supplies are not meant for children under 13 to use. If you're not sure if something is safe for you to use, ask an adult if it's okay. When using craft supplies that have a strong odour, work in a room that has plenty of fresh air. If an object is difficult to cut, ask an adult to help.

Jewellery-Making Tips

To make it easier to thread beads on thread or wool, dab some glue on the end of the thread and allow it to dry. The end will be stiff so the beads will slide on more easily.

Make sure the holes in your beads are large enough to take the thread, string or elastic you're using.

After tying a knot to finish off a necklace or bracelet, dab some glue on the knot to help stop it unravelling.

To protect a painted finish, you can brush some PVA glue over it and leave it to dry.

MAKING A SQUARE KNOT

You can use this knot to tie the ends of elastic together. Once you tie the knot, trim off the ends.

STEP 1

Make a simple overhand knot by bringing the ends together and feeding the left end over the right.

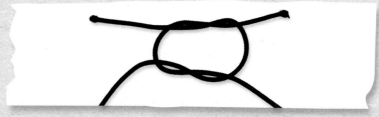

STEP 2

Make another overhand knot in the opposite direction, with the right end over the left end.

BLANKET STITCH

The blanket stitch is often used to decorate the edge of fabric items, especially blankets. As well as using it for the felt purse on pages 42–43, you can use it around the edges of felt flowers or to decorate other items, such as belts and handbags. Embroidery thread works best, and you will need a sewing needle with a large eye.

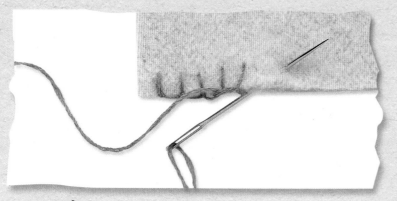

STEP 1

To start, insert the needle through the back of the fabric to the front at the very bottom edge. Bring the needle up through the back of the fabric about 5 to 10 millimetres away diagonally.

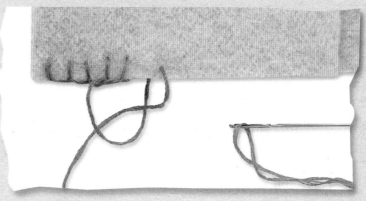

STEP 2

Bring your needle straight down, making sure the needle goes through the loop of thread. Pull the thread until it is tight – but not so tight the fabric bunches up.

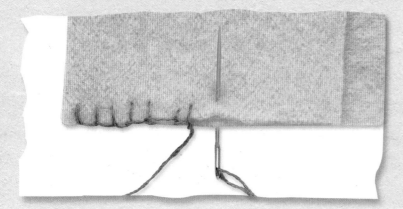

STEP 3

Take the needle to the back again and make the next stitch 5 to 10 millimetres away from the first stitch. Continue in this way until you finish the edge. Each new stitch will hold the loop of the previous stitch.

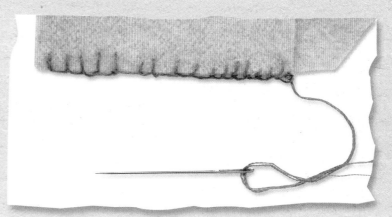

STEP 4

At the end, take your thread to the back over the last loop to secure it. Make a small stitch in the back of the fabric and knot it.

Cute as a button

Buttons come in all sort of shapes, sizes and colours, from tiny, plain buttons to colourful buttons shaped like animals. Save up lots of buttons to have plenty of choice when making a bracelet.

YOU WILL NEED:
....
elastic, scissors, buttons

STEP 1
Cut a piece of elastic that will fit around your wrist twice, with about 12 centimetres extra. Fold the elastic in half, and tie a knot in the folded end to form a small loop.

STEP 2
Feed the buttons one at a time onto the elastic, with one end of the elastic in each hole – the buttons should stand next to each other. Vary the colours of the buttons.

STEP 3
Continue feeding the buttons onto the elastic until only 5 centimetres are left at the end of the elastic.

STEP 4
Thread the ends of the elastic through the loop and tie a knot. Tie a pair of buttons to the ends as a finishing touch.

STEP 1

For a bracelet with fewer buttons, cut some elastic that fits around your wrist twice, with 12 centimetres extra. Fold the elastic in half; tie a knot in the end to make a small loop.

STEP 2

Thread both ends of the elastic through both of the holes in each button, so that the buttons lie flat. Slide the buttons together.

STEP 3

Continue threading the buttons onto the elastic until only 5 centimetres are left at the end of the elastic.

STEP 4

Thread the ends of the elastic through the loop at the folded end, and tie a knot and bow.

Buttons that are the same size, with two holes, are the easiest to use.

These buttons are all the same size, but for the bracelet with the flat buttons you can use one larger button as a centrepiece for your bracelet.

Friends forever

You'll only need string and beads to make this fun bracelet. Why not make two matching bracelets – one for yourself and one to give to your best friend as a friendship bracelet.

YOU WILL NEED:
•••••••••••••••••••••••••••••••••
string, ruler, PVA glue, beads, scissors

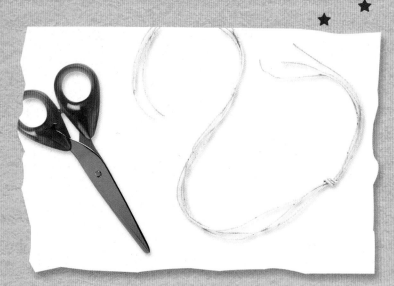

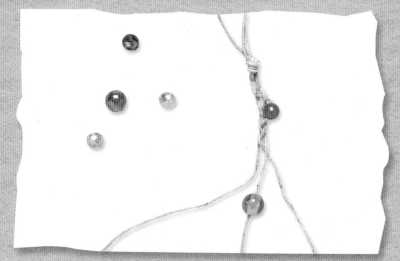

STEP 1

Cut three pieces of string 50 centimetres long. Tie them together, making a knot 10 centimetres from one end. To help thread on beads, dab the ends in glue; let dry.

STEP 2

Ask a friend to hold the knot (or hold it in the clip on a clipboard) and begin plaiting – weave the strings over and under each other. Thread on a bead every few centimetres.

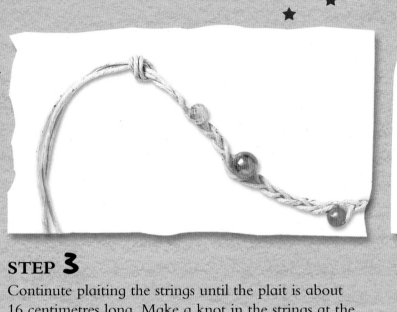

STEP 3

Continute plaiting the strings until the plait is about 16 centimetres long. Make a knot in the strings at the end of the plait – make sure you pull it tightly.

STEP 4

Thread a bead onto the end of a string and make a knot under the bead. Cut off the extra string. Repeat for all the strings – try to keep the lengths the same.

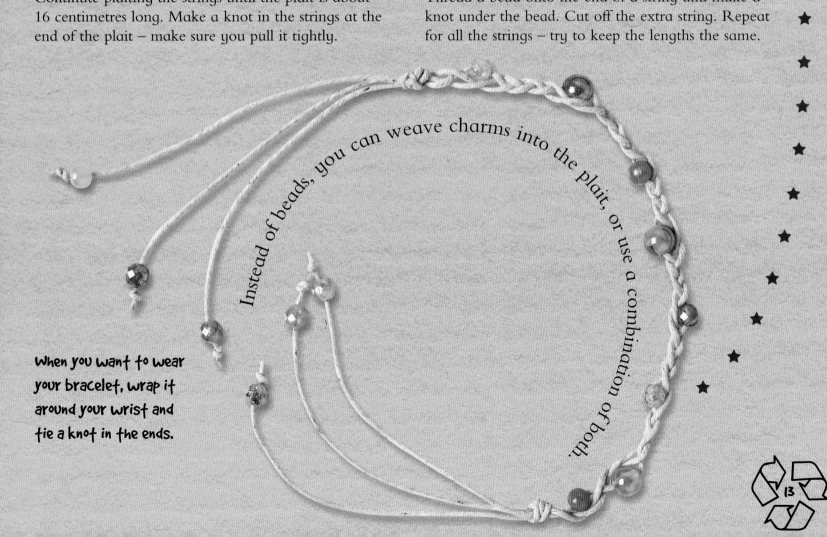

Instead of beads, you can weave charms into the plait, or use a combination of both.

When you want to wear your bracelet, wrap it around your wrist and tie a knot in the ends.

13

Nice 'n' easy

Everyday plastic drinking straws can be turned into a cool anklet that's ideal for wearing at the beach. If you have pierced ears, make the matching earrings, too. Don't forget to wash the straws and let them dry before using them.

YOU WILL NEED:
•••••••••••••••••••••••••••••
straws, scissors, elastic, earring fastenings, thread, beads

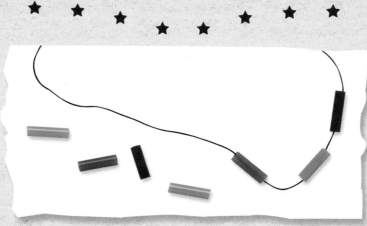

STEP 1

For the anklet, cut several different-coloured straws into short lengths, about 1 to 2 centimetres long.

STEP 2

Cut a length of elastic that will fit around your ankle, with a few centimetres extra. Thread the short pieces of straw onto the elastic – make sure they don't slip off the end as you thread them on.

STEP 3

After threading on the straw pieces, tie the ends together into a square knot (see page 8), then trim off the extra elastic.

14

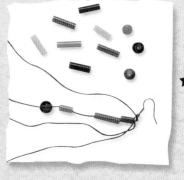

STEP 1

For each earring, cut two lengths of thread, about 8 to 10 centimetres long. Thread them halfway through an earring fastening and tie a knot.

STEP 2

Cut some straws into pieces about 1 centimetre long. If you want the earrings to match the anklet, use straws that are the same colours.

STEP 3

Thread some of the straw pieces onto each length of thread, add a bead at the end and tie a knot around the bead. Cut off any extra thread.

Use the same pattern of colours as shown here, or choose your own colour scheme.

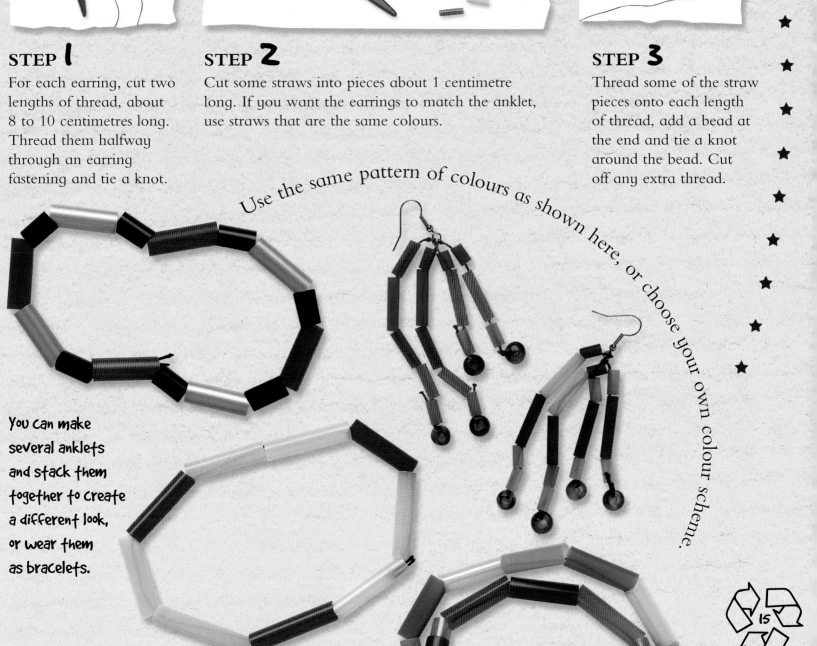

You can make several anklets and stack them together to create a different look, or wear them as bracelets.

15

Silvery sparklers

Here's a great way to turn safety pins into jewellery. You can make a groovy bracelet and brooch that will be the envy of your friends. Use safety pins that are all the same size to make the bracelet. You'll need only one large safety pin to make the brooch.

YOU WILL NEED:
medium or large safety pins, small beads, hat elastic, one large safety pin, fine ribbon and thonging, charms

ECOFACT
Safety pins are made from steel and can be recycled, but reusing them will mean saving the energy needed to recycle them. If you have a new shirt, jumper or dress, save and reuse any safety pins attaching a label or button to it.

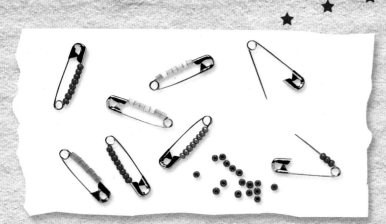

STEP 1

For the bracelet, thread small beads onto the spike of a safety pin to 5 millimetres from the tip. Close the pin. Do this for each safety pin you're using.

STEP 2

Cut a 50-centimetre-long piece of hat elastic in half. Insert one length through the top fastening part of one safety pin, then through the ring at the bottom of the next safety pin, with the beads facing outwards.

16

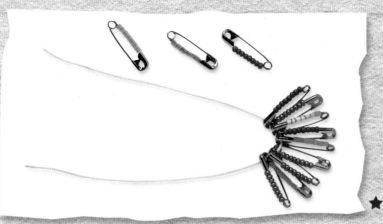

STEP 3

Continue threading the safety pins onto the elastic, following the same pattern of threading through the top part of one safety pin, then the ring at the bottom of the next safety pin. Make sure the beads face outwards.

STEP 4

Wrap the bracelet around your wrist so that the first and last safety pin are side by side, and check the fit. Add or remove safety pins if necessary. Tie the elastic ends together in a square knot (see page 8). Cut off the extra elastic.

STEP 5

Thread the other piece of elastic through the holes at the other end of the safety pins. Tie the elastic ends together in a square knot. Cut off the extra elastic.

Silvery sparklers

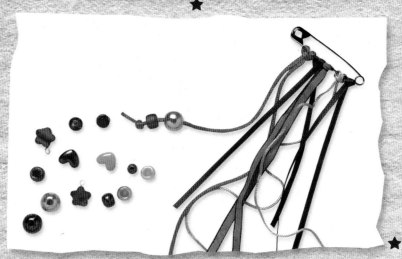

STEP 1

For the brooch, cut thonging and ribbon into lengths 10 to 12 centimetres long. Fold a length in half. Push the folded end through the safety pin. Feed the ends through the loop and pull. Repeat for all the lengths.

STEP 2

Thread pink and lilac beads (make sure they have large holes) and flower-shaped charms onto the ribbon and thonging.

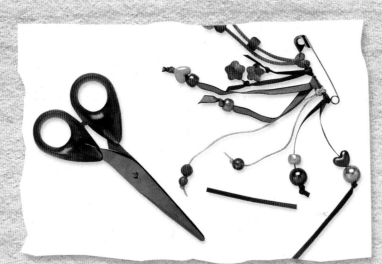

STEP 3

Tie knots in the ribbon and thonging under the beads and charms so that they hang at different levels. Make sure the knots are large enough so that the beads and charms do not slip off. Cut off the extra ribbon and thonging.

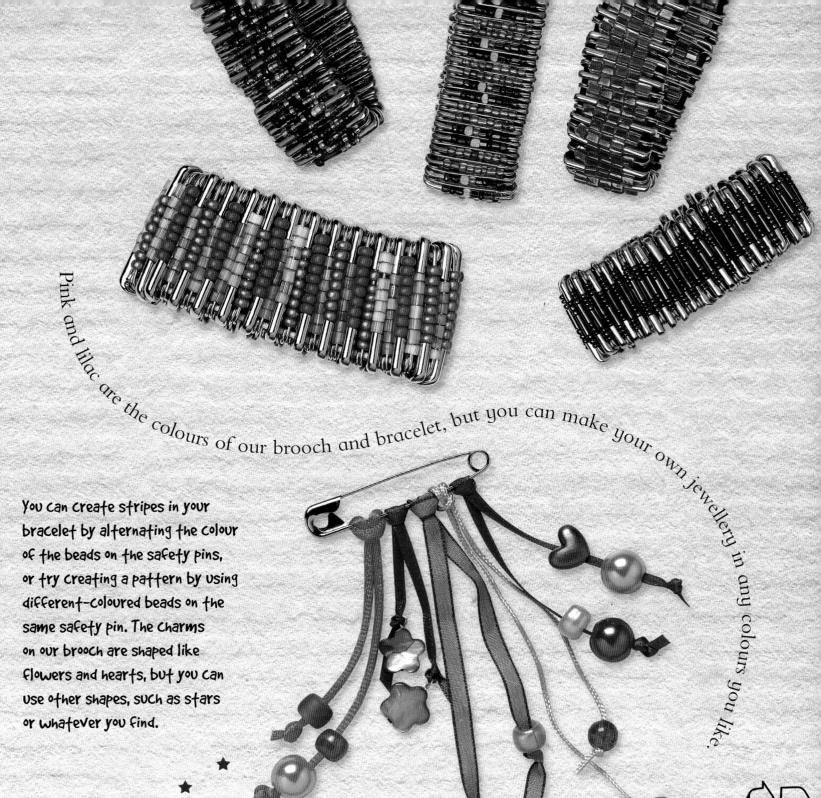

Pink and lilac are the colours of our brooch and bracelet, but you can make your own jewellery in any colours you like.

You can create stripes in your bracelet by alternating the colour of the beads on the safety pins, or try creating a pattern by using different-coloured beads on the same safety pin. The charms on our brooch are shaped like flowers and hearts, but you can use other shapes, such as stars or whatever you find.

Flower power

Make your own corsage with leftover scraps of fabric. It will make any party dress look extra special when pinned on with a safety pin – or try sewing the back of it onto a ribbon to tie it around your wrist.

YOU WILL NEED:
two contrasting fabric scraps, paper, pencil, ruler, scissors, button, thread, needle, safety pin

STEP 1
Make two templates for different-sized flowers. Cut a 10-centimetre square and an 11-centimetre square from some paper.

STEP 2
Fold a square in half along one side, then in half along the other side. Find the corner where the two folds meet. Above it, draw the shape of one petal.

STEP 3
Using a pair of scissors, cut along your outline – be careful not to cut into the folded corner. Unfold the paper and a flower will appear. Repeat for the second template.

STEP 4
Use the large template to cut two flower shapes from a dark-coloured fabric and one flower shape from a lighter-coloured fabric.

20

STEP 5

Use the small template to cut a shape each from the dark-coloured fabric and the light-coloured fabric.

STEP 6

Place all the flower shapes one on top of the other, in alternating colours and with the petals staggered.

STEP 7

Thread a needle, tie a knot at the end and feed a button onto the thread. Push the needle through the centre of the petals, with the button at the top. Sew the button on tightly.

STEP 8

Gather the petals together, with the button inside, and wrap the thread above the button a few times. Tie a knot in the thread and cut off the extra thread.

You can use different colour combinations when making your own corsage.

Attach the safety pin to the back of the corsage so you can wear the flower on your dress. The fabric for our orange and yellow corsage is plain, but you can also use fabric that has a pretty pattern on it.

21

Chunky funky beads

You can make your very own beads by using pages from a magazine or other glossy paper. Choose the most colourful sections to create the best beads, and use the beads to make original necklaces and bracelets.

YOU WILL NEED:
....
magazine or glossy paper, ruler, pen, scissors, glue, paintbrush, knitting needle, elastic

Once you cut out one triangle, use it to trace around and make the others.

STEP 1
Cut out long triangle shapes from a magazine. They should be at least 16 centimetres long to make chunky beads, and about 2 centimetres wide at the base. You can use a ruler and pen to make an outline of the shape on the paper.

STEP 2
Spread some glue on a triangle, from the point to about three-fourths of the way towards the wide base – leave the end at the base unglued.

STEP 3
Wrap the triangle around a knitting needle. Start at the base so you don't get glue on the needle. When you reach the end of the triangle, press it down.

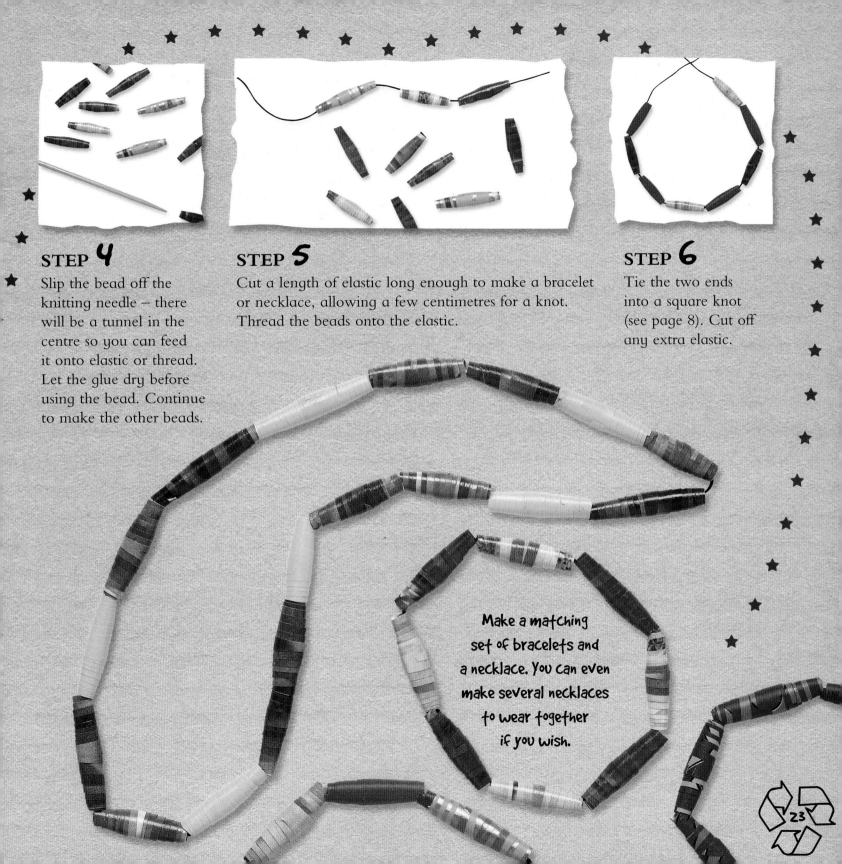

STEP 4

Slip the bead off the knitting needle – there will be a tunnel in the centre so you can feed it onto elastic or thread. Let the glue dry before using the bead. Continue to make the other beads.

STEP 5

Cut a length of elastic long enough to make a bracelet or necklace, allowing a few centimetres for a knot. Thread the beads onto the elastic.

STEP 6

Tie the two ends into a square knot (see page 8). Cut off any extra elastic.

Make a matching set of bracelets and a necklace. You can even make several necklaces to wear together if you wish.

Picture perfect

You can turn plastic bottle lids into your own special jewellery. We're using them on a necklace, but you can also make them into a bracelet, brooch or earrings.

YOU WILL NEED:
••••••••••••••••••••••••••••••••••••••
two small plastic bottle lids, one large plastic bottle lid, wrapping paper, pencil, thin ribbon, scissors, PVA glue, paintbrush

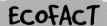

ECOFACT

Although many types of plastic bottles can be recycled, their lids cannot. They are made of a different type of plastic, which is why they must be removed from a bottle before it is recycled. Instead of sending bottle lids to the landfill, try thinking of ways to reuse them.

STEP 1

Choose sections of the wrapping paper to cut out. You can use the lids as templates and trace around them with a pencil, but cut out circles a little smaller than the lids.

STEP 2

Cut a length of thin ribbon long enough to fit around your neck once it is tied. Ask a grown-up to cut a pair of slits into the top of each bottle lid with a scalpel knife.

24

STEP 3

Carefully feed the ribbon through the slits in the bottle lids, placing the largest lid in the middle. You may need to ask an adult to push the ribbon through with a thin knitting needle or other pointy item.

STEP 4

Centre the lids on the ribbon. Once you are happy with their position, glue the cut-out pictures into the lids. The pictures will also be glued to the ribbon, so you won't be able to move the lids. Let the glue dry.

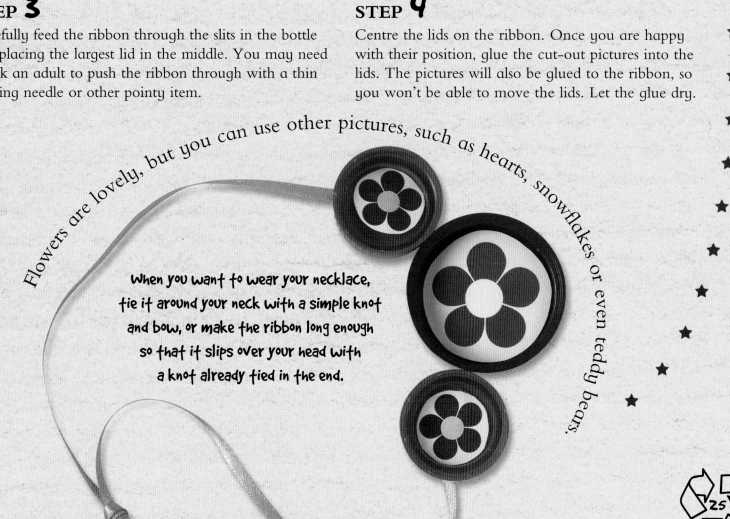

Flowers are lovely, but you can use other pictures, such as hearts, snowflakes or even teddy bears.

When you want to wear your necklace, tie it around your neck with a simple knot and bow, or make the ribbon long enough so that it slips over your head with a knot already tied in the end.

It's a stick-up

For girls with long hair, what better way of keeping it up than using a pair of Oriental-style hair sticks. The next time you have a Chinese takeaway, save the chopsticks. Wash them and let them dry before you make the hair sticks.

YOU WILL NEED:
••
chopsticks, gems, PVA glue, paintbrush, ribbon, scissors, beads, magazine or wrapping paper, ruler, pen, gold paint

STEP 1

For sparkling gem hair sticks, glue some gems along the wider end of the chopsticks, adding them to all four sides and using the same colours on both sticks for a matching pair. Choose a pair of large gems and glue one to the end of each chopstick. Allow the glue to dry.

STEP 2

Cut two lengths of thin, colourful ribbon, about 10 centimetres long. Thread a bead onto each end of the ribbons and tie knots at the ends.

STEP 3

Tie a ribbon onto each chopstick, towards the end of the stick. You can wrap it around the stick two or three times.

STEP 1

For paper-bead hair sticks, use a ruler and pen to make outlines for two triangles, each one 40 centimetres long and 2 centimetres wide at the base, on a colourful piece of a magazine (or wrapping paper). Cut them out. Paint two 1-centimetre bands of gold on the chopsticks – one at the top and one 5 centimetres below the first one. Allow the paint to dry.

STEP 2

Spread glue on the back of a triangle, completely covering it. Wrap it around the chopstick near the top – just by the paint – starting with the base of the triangle.

STEP 3

Wrap the second triangle below the first one. Once the glue is dry, you have your beads. Cover them with glue to give them a really shiny finish.

The chopstick hair sticks are ready to wear in your hair. You can use curled ribbon to decorate a pair of hair sticks, or try adding sparkling gems to the top of the hair sticks decorated with beads.

27

My little ponytail

Any girl with long hair will love this special hair clip. It will add colour and fun when your hair is pulled back in a ponytail.

YOU WILL NEED:
cardboard tube, ruler, pencil, scissors, lollipop stick, tissue paper, PVA glue, paintbrush, striped paper, button, pair of compasses, needle, thread, sticky tape, felt-tipped pens

STEP 1
Cut a 4-centimetre-wide ring from a cardboard tube. Cut through the ring, then measure along 10 centimetres from the first cut, and cut again to make a 10 x 4-centimetre piece of curved card.

STEP 2
Carefully snip out a slit at either end of the card (you might need to ask a grown-up to help). These should be big enough to slide the lollipop stick through.

STEP 3
Cut a piece of tissue paper bigger than the card. Scrunch it up to make wrinkles, then smooth it out. Brush glue onto the front of the card and stick the tissue on it. Cut off the corners. Fold the sides in and glue to the back.

STEP 4
Add another two or three layers of tissue paper in the same way. Push the end of the scissors through the slits in the card so they don't get covered. Brush some glue all over the card, then leave to dry thoroughly.

STEP 5

Draw a heart onto stripy paper and cut it out. Brush glue onto the back of the heart. Stick it to the centre of the hair clip, cover it with glue and leave to dry.

STEP 6

Put a button on top of the heart. Mark through the holes with a pencil. Remove the button, then make holes at the marks, using a pair of compasses.

STEP 7

Sew the button on, taking your needle and thread through the holes in the button and the card. Make a knot at the back and cover it with tape.

STEP 8

Use felt pens to draw stripes onto a lollipop stick, starting with light colours. Allow to dry, then brush glue all over to seal it. Leave to dry.

Slide the stick through the slits in your hair clip to hold your ponytail in place. You can use patterned paper instead of tissue paper, or add a felt flower with a sparkly gem.

By scrunching up the tissue paper, you will create a cool wrinkly texture.

29

Little charmers

A dangling charm hanging from your key ring will impress your friends and make it easier to spot your keys. You can also use the charm to decorate your school bag, or even your mobile phone.

YOU WILL NEED:
wool, PVA glue, paintbrush, scissors, buttons, key ring

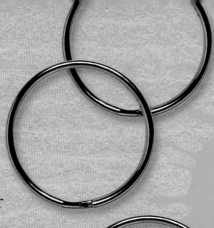

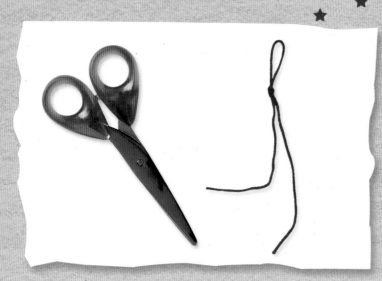

STEP 1

Cut a length of wool 30 centimetres long. Fold the length in half, and make a knot about 2.5 centimetres from the folded end.

STEP 2

Dab some glue onto the cut ends of the wool to prevent it from unravelling. Make sure the glue has dried before you move on to the next step.

STEP 3

Thread the buttons onto the wool by threading each end of the wool through a separate hole in the buttons.

STEP 4

Tie a square knot (see page 8) in the wool under the last button. Cut off the extra wool, but leave a tassle.

For the best result, experiment with the arrangement of the buttons before you tie the knot at the end.

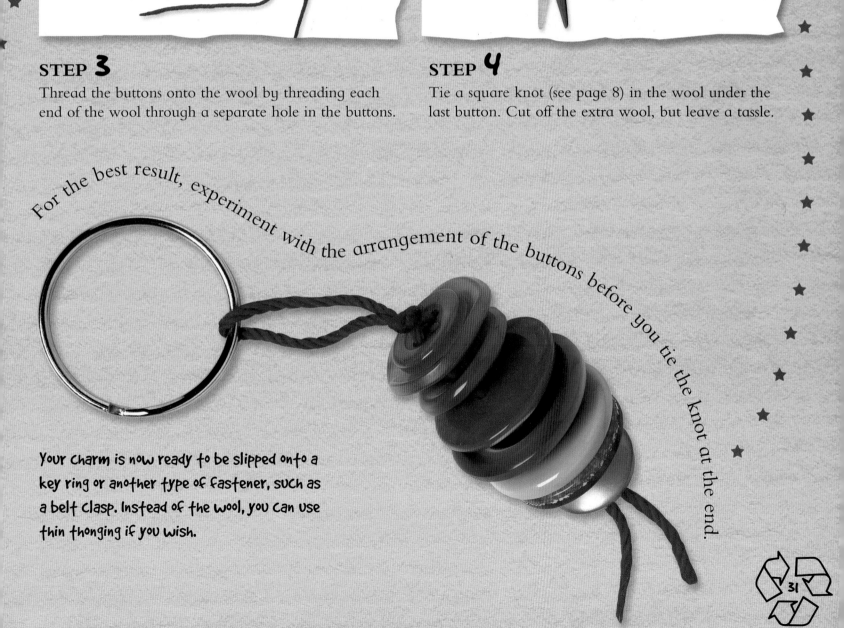

Your charm is now ready to be slipped onto a key ring or another type of fastener, such as a belt clasp. Instead of the wool, you can use thin thonging if you wish.

Plastic fantastic

No one will guess that this clever belt is made from plastic carrier bags! For a longer belt, make two woven sections and join them together with a bangle or curtain ring.

YOU WILL NEED:
. . . .
two small bangles or curtain rings, PVA glue, paintbrush, thread, scissors, plastic carrier bags in four different colours, ruler, tape, paperclip, sticky-backed plastic, beads, needle

STEP 1

For each bangle or curtain ring, dab a blob of glue on it. Stick the end of your thread down in the glue, and wrap it tightly and evenly around the bangle. Cut off the end and add a small blob of glue to hold it in place.

STEP 2

Cut seven strips of carrier bag, 3.5 centimetres wide and long enough to fit around your waist. You will need two strips each of the first colour, second and third colours, and one strip of the fourth colour.

STEP 3

Tape the strips together at one end. Arrange them in this order: first colour, second colour, third colour, fourth colour, third colour, second colour, first colour.

STEP 4

Take the left-hand strip and weave it over the strip next to it, then under the next strip and over the following one.

STEP 5

Repeat step 4, but this time start with the strip on the right-hand side. As before, weave the end strip over the strip next to it, then under the next strip and over the following one.

STEP 6

You should now have a new colour on both the right- and left-hand sides. Weave these into the centre in the same way (over, under, over) as in steps 4 and 5.

Plastic fantastic

STEP 7

Keep weaving until you reach the end of the strips. Hold them in place with a paperclip. Cut the ends of the strips so they are all even.

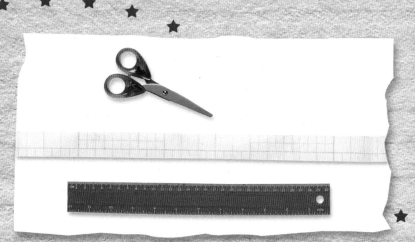

STEP 8

Cut a piece of sticky-backed plastic 3 centimetres wide and as long as your belt.

STEP 9

Fold the taped end of the woven strip around a thread–wrapped ring. Stick it in place by pressing an end of the sticky-backed plastic strip, sticky-side down, firmly against the woven strip.

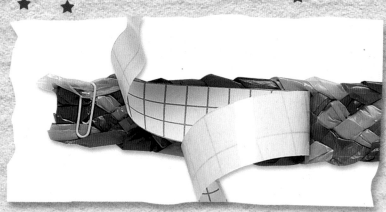

STEP 10

Gradually peel the backing off the rest of the sticky-backed plastic strip and press it into place along the back of the woven strip. Stop several centimetres short of the paperclipped end.

STEP 11

Fold the end around a ring and remove the clip. Stick the plastic over the end, trimming off any extra.

STEP 12

Choose one or two of the colours, and cut four more carrier bag strips 45 and 55 centimetres long. Fold them in half and loop two around each of the thread-wrapped rings.

STEP 13

For each strip, thread it through a needle, add some beads onto the end and tie a knot under the last bead.

These belts are fun to make. You can also use thicker plastic strips and make a simple plait, or make your own rings by cutting circles from thick card and painting them.

35

Ring-a-ding-ding

Wooden or plastic curtain rings held together with ribbon or thonging will make a really funky belt. We've used 11 curtain rings to create this belt, but you can adjust the size of your belt to fit you by adding more rings or using fewer of them.

YOU WILL NEED:

curtain rings, acrylic paint, paintbrush, thonging or ribbon, scissors

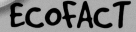

ECOFACT

Curtain rings, whether plastic or wooden, can be reused over and over again, even if the curtains are replaced. However, if the curtain rings are taken down, save them to reuse in another way. If you remove the metal eyes, save the eyes to reuse them, too.

STEP 1

Paint dots on the curtain rings and leave to dry. Turn them over and paint dots on the other side.

STEP 2

Once the paint is dry, unscrew the metal eyes from the rings. You may need an adult to help if they are in too tight.

STEP 3

Cut 10 lengths of thonging, each one approximately 25 centimetres long. You'll need about 4 metres of thonging in total, including an extra piece to be used to tie the belt together.

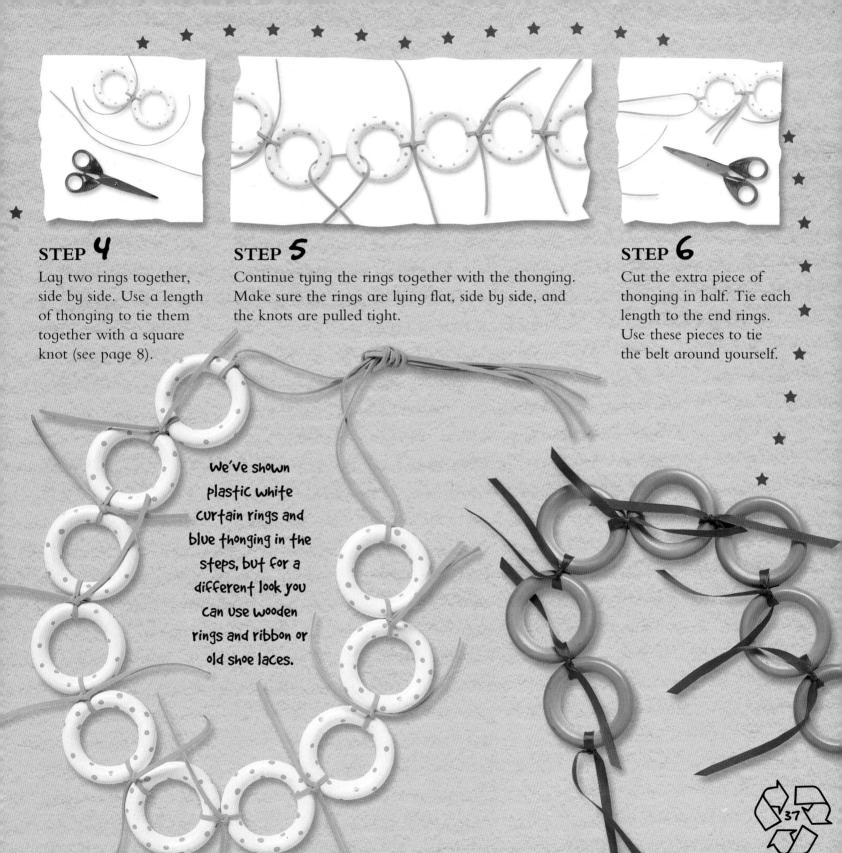

STEP 4

Lay two rings together, side by side. Use a length of thonging to tie them together with a square knot (see page 8).

STEP 5

Continue tying the rings together with the thonging. Make sure the rings are lying flat, side by side, and the knots are pulled tight.

STEP 6

Cut the extra piece of thonging in half. Tie each length to the end rings. Use these pieces to tie the belt around yourself.

We've shown plastic white curtain rings and blue thonging in the steps, but for a different look you can use wooden rings and ribbon or old shoe laces.

Wrapped and ready

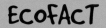

Save scraps of wrapping paper to make this terrific handbag. You'll also need some denim, so this is a perfect way to reuse denim pieces left over if you've cut off jeans to make shorts!

ECOFACT

The paper industry is the UK's largest recycler, with two-thirds of the industry taking part in recycling. You can help by buying wrapping paper made from recycled paper, and use ribbon to wrap it around a present instead of tape. The paper won't be damaged and can be used again.

YOU WILL NEED:
metallic wrapping paper, ruler, pencil, scissors, piece of denim jeans or skirt, chalk, PVA glue, paintbrush, ribbon, large needle, Velcro

STEP 1
To make a folded strip, cut a 7-centimetre x 17-centimetre rectangle from wrapping paper. Fold it in half lengthways and crease along the fold.

STEP 2
Unfold the paper. Then fold both of the long edges in so they meet the crease in the centre. Press firmly along the folds so that they make creases.

STEP 3
Fold the paper along the centre crease again, making a narrow strip. (The long cut edges should now be hidden inside the strip.)

STEP 4
Next, fold the strip in half widthways. Press firmly along the fold to make a crease, then unfold the last fold made in the paper.

STEP 5

Bring the short ends to the middle so that they meet the centre crease. Fold the strip in half one last time.

STEP 6

This is your first finished piece, and it should be a 'V' shape. Repeat steps 1 to 5 to make additional folded strips.

STEP 7

The strip makes two loops. To join two folded strips together, slide one open end of one strip through each of these loops.

STEP 8

Make and add a third folded strip in the same way, and keep going to create a chain with 24 strips. Make five chains.

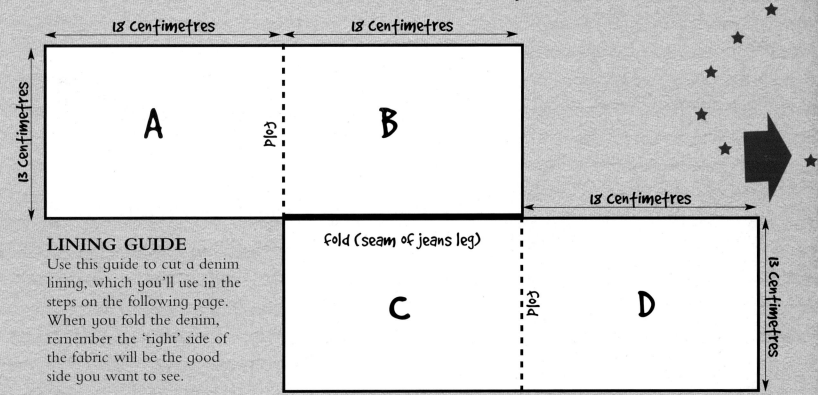

18 Centimetres — 18 Centimetres

13 Centimetres

A   fold   B

LINING GUIDE

Use this guide to cut a denim lining, which you'll use in the steps on the following page. When you fold the denim, remember the 'right' side of the fabric will be the good side you want to see.

18 Centimetres

fold (seam of jeans leg)

13 Centimetres

C   fold   D

39

Wrapped and ready

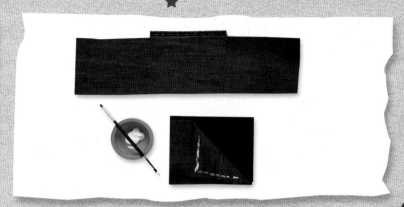

★ STEP 9

Cut out the bag lining from a scrap piece of denim. Using the guide on page 39, make an outline on the fabric with chalk. Make sure there is a seam running through the centre of the fabric.

STEP 10

Fold the lining in half along the seam. Tuck the sides inside and glue them, with the right side of section A against the wrong side of section C, and the right side of section D against the wrong side of section B.

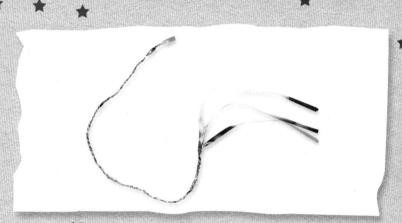

STEP 11

Glue a chain of strips onto the lining so the points hide the bottom edge. Fold over at the sides and overlap the chain ends. Glue on the other chains to hide the denim.

STEP 12

Cut three lengths of ribbon 240 centimetres long, and knot them together at one end. Plait all three lengths together, weaving them under and over each other.

STEP 13

Use a needle to thread the plaited strand into one side of the bag and out the other side of the bag. Tie the ends together.

STEP 14

Cut a 7-centimetre x 9-centimetre piece of wrapping paper. Fold the long edges into the middle. Glue them down.

STEP 15

Adjust the plaited strap so the knot is at the top (it will sit on your shoulder). Wrap and glue the paper strip around the knot to hide it.

STEP 16

Cut two small pieces of Velcro and glue them just inside the top edge of the bag to make a closure. Your bag is ready to use.

You can use colourful magazine pages or sweet wrappers instead of using wrapping paper, or make a smaller chain and wear it as a cute bracelet.

My little purse

An old wool jumper can be made into felt, which you can make into your own purse. Ask an adult to wash the woolly item on the hottest cycle in a washing machine. Let the felted wool dry before you use it.

YOU WILL NEED:
• •
old wool jumper or other woolly item, paper, pencil, ruler, scissors, straight pins, sewing needle, embroidery thread, button, string, scraps of felt

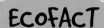

ECOFACT

In the USA, more than 3.6 million tonnes of clothes and fabrics are put out in the rubbish each year, with most of it going to landfills. Before industrialization in the 19th century, women had to spin thread and weave fabric by hand, so every scrap of fabric was saved and used.

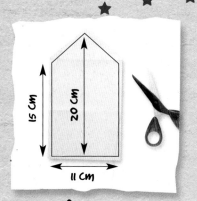

15 CM · 20 CM · 11 CM

STEP 1
Cut a sheet of paper into a shape 11 centimetres long at the base, 20 centimetres long in the centre and 15 centimetres at the sides.

STEP 2
Pin your paper template to the felted wool, then cut around it. Be careful to keep the edges straight. Unpin the paper, and put it aside to reuse elsewhere.

STEP 3
Fold the bottom half of the rectangle up to the base of the triangle and pin it in place. Thread a needle with a length of embroidery thread.

STEP 4
Using a blanket stitch (see page 9), sew up one side and continue to the point of the triangle; leave some extra thread. Repeat on the other side.

42

STEP 5

Cut a piece of string long enough to make a loop that a button will fit in. Use the extra thread to sew on the loop. Fold the flap down. Use the loop to position the button, then sew it on.

STEP 6

Cut out two flower shapes, one smaller than the other, from some scrap pieces of felt. For a really cute flower, use two different colours.

STEP 7

Assemble the flower with the larger flower on the bottom and a button on top of the smaller flower. Turn the flower shapes so the petals don't overlap.

STEP 8

Sew the flower shapes together, with the button. Now you can sew the flower onto the purse.

A contrasting colour will make the blanket stitch stand out and create a funky border around the purse.

Instead of the flower, you can decorate your purse by sewing on a border of buttons or gluing on gems or sequins.

Flowers and jewels

Open the lid of this pretty box to discover flower petals showing off your jewellery. When you do the papier-mâché, tear the pieces. The ripped edges will smooth into each other, creating a nice, neat finish.

YOU WILL NEED:
• •

thick card, ruler, pencil, scissors, parcel tape, tape, kitchen paper or tissue paper, wallpaper paste, paint, paintbrush, felt, PVA glue, cardboard tubes, kitchen sponge, envelopes (with patterns printed inside), thin card, black pen, two buttons

ECOFACT

An average family uses three rolls of kitchen paper a week. If each home in the USA used one roll of kitchen paper made from recycled paper instead of 'virgin', or new, paper, 864,000 trees and 1.3 billion litres of water would be saved. That's enough water to supply more than 10,000 families for a year.

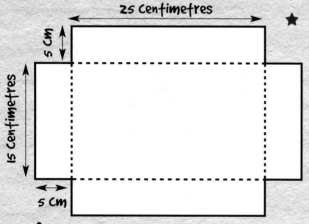

STEP 1

Use the template above as a guide to draw the box sections onto thick card. Cut out the outline of the box with scissors.

STEP 2

Ask an adult to score along the dotted lines marked on the template, cutting into the line with the blade of the scissors but without cutting through the card.

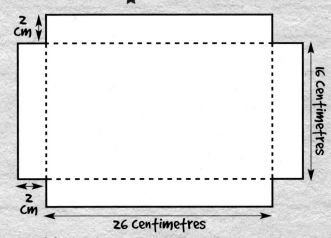

STEP 3

Fold each of the four sides up and inwards. Then use parcel tape to hold them together at the edges and create your box shape.

STEP 4

Make the lid of your box, following the second template above. Draw the lid onto thick card and cut out the outline of the lid. Ask an adult to score along the dotted lines.

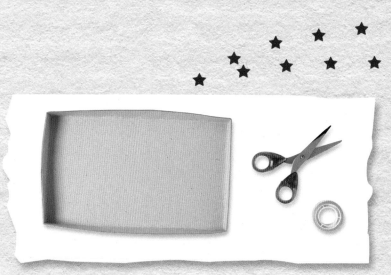

STEP 5

Fold each of the four sides up and inwards. Then use regular sticky tape to hold the sides together at the edges and create your lid shape.

STEP 6

Papier-mâché your box by tearing kitchen paper or tissue paper into pieces. Dip one piece at a time into wallpaper paste. Cover the outside of the main box, wrapping the pasted paper over the top edge. Cover the whole of the lid, inside and outside.

Flowers and jewels

STEP 7

When the papier-mâché is dry, paint the bottom of the box green and the top pale pink. Leave to dry.

STEP 8

Cut some pink felt to fit inside the base of the box and around the sides. Glue each piece carefully into place inside the box. (To make your own felt, see page 42.)

STEP 9

Cut seven sections from a cardboard tube, each one about 3.5 centimetres wide. Paint six of them pale pink and the last one bright pink.

STEP 10

Draw around the bottom of the bright pink tube onto the sponge (remove the backing if it has one) and cut out the shape. Cut three slits into the top of the sponge circle (to hold rings). Brush glue inside the cardboard tube, then slip the sponge into it.

STEP 11

Arrange the tubes inside the box in a flower shape, with the bright pink tube in the centre. Picking up one tube at a time, spread a thin line of glue around the bottom edge and press it down onto the felt.

STEP 12

Pick five envelopes with different patterns inside. Water down some of the bright pink paint so it is runny. Brush the paint inside the envelopes (the patterns should show through). Leave to dry.

STEP 13

Draw a large and a small petal shape onto a scrap of card and cut out. Draw around each one five times onto the painted envelopes; cut out the shapes. Outline the petals with a black pen.

STEP 14

Glue the petals in a circle to the top of the box lid, with the smaller petals just below the big ones. Stick a plain button on top of each circle to make a flower centre.

If you've got lots of rings, try filling more of the cardboard tube flower petals with pieces of kitchen sponge. You could also recycle scraps of foam to make your ring holders. foam is sometimes found in packaging.

47

Index